Meet **Desert**
ANIMALS

CAMELS

by Rose Davin

CAPSTONE PRESS
a capstone imprint

Pebble Plus is published by Capstone Press,
1710 Roe Crest Drive, North Mankato, Minnesota 56003
www.mycapstone.com

Library of Congress Cataloging-in-Publication Data
Names: Davin, Rose, author.
Title: Camels / by Rose Davin.
Description: North Mankato, Minnesota : Capstone Press, a Capstone imprint, [2017] |
Series: Pebble plus. Meet desert animals | Audience: Ages 4–8. | Audience: K to grade 3.
 | Includes bibliographical references and index.
Identifiers: LCCN 2016035493 | ISBN 9781515746003 (library binding) | ISBN
 9781515746072 (pbk.) | ISBN 9781515746256 (eBook PDF)
Subjects: LCSH: Camels—Juvenile literature.
Classification: LCC QL737.U54 D365 2017 | DDC 599.63/62—dc23
LC record available at https://lccn.loc.gov/2016035493

Editorial Credits
Marysa Storm and Alesha Sullivan, editors; Kayla Rossow, designer;
Ruth Smith, media researcher; Kathy McColley, production specialist

Photo Credits
Capstone Press: 6; Dreamstime: © Aleksandr Frolov, 21; Shutterstock: Asian Images, 2,
24, David Steele, 19, Don Mammoser, 17, Gillian Holliday, cover, back cover, Hitdelight,
24, Maxim Petrichuk, 9 muznabutt, 7, Naiyyer, 11, Olena Tur, 5, optionm, 22, schankz, 13,
Wolfgang Zwanzger, 1, YANGCHAO, 15

Note to Parents and Teachers

The Meet Desert Animals set supports national curriculum standards for science
related to life science and ecosystems. This book describes and illustrates camels. The
images support early readers in understanding the text. The repetition of words and
phrases helps early readers learn new words. This book also introduces early readers
to subject-specific vocabulary words, which are defined in the Glossary section. Early
readers may need assistance to read some words and to use the Table of Contents,
Glossary, Read More, Internet Sites, Critical Thinking Using the Common Core, and
Index sections of the book.

Printed and bound in China.
007872

TABLE OF CONTENTS

WOOLY WORKERS

Camels roll in the desert sand.

They nap in the hot sun.

But camels work too. They carry

people and heavy loads.

Most camels live in deserts in Africa and Asia. Camels follow one another across the sand. They stay together in groups called herds.

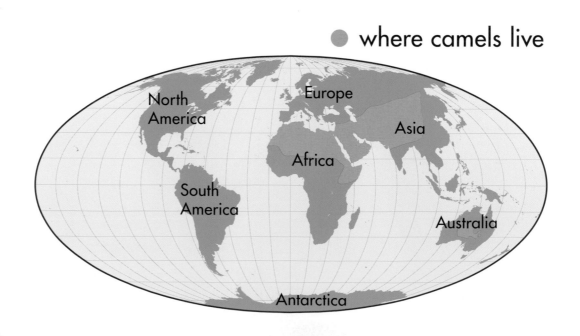

● where camels live

North America

Europe

Asia

Africa

South America

Australia

Antarctica

FROM HEAD TO TOE

Camels have one or two humps.

The humps store fat. Their bodies

use the fat when they can't find food.

Bactrian camel

During sandstorms camels can close their nostrils. This keeps sand out. Their long eyelashes keep sand out of their eyes.

TIME TO EAT

Camels are not picky eaters. They nibble on any desert plants they can find. Wild onions are some of their favorites.

Camels can go for months without water.

Thirsty camels can drink about 30 gallons

(100 liters) of water in 10 minutes.

Slurp!

LIFE CYCLE

Female camels usually have one calf every two years. Calves can walk on the day they are born. They drink their mothers' milk for about one year.

Young camels stay with their family
herd for about four years.

Camels can live more than 40 years.

Glossary

calf—a young camel

desert—a dry area of land with few plants; deserts receive very little rain

herd—a large group of animals that lives or moves together

hump—the raised rounded area on the back of a camel; camel humps are filled with fat

nostril—an opening in the nose used to breathe and smell

Read More

Morey, Allan. *Camels are Awesome.* Awesome Asian Animals. North Mankato, Minn.: Capstone Press, 2016.

Oblinger, Mark. *Camels Close Their Noses: Desert Animals.* Minneapolis: Cantata Learning, 2016.

Riggs, Kate. *Camels.* Amazing Animals. Mankato, Minn.: Creative Education, 2014.

Internet Sites

FactHound offers a safe, fun way to find Internet sites related to this book. All of the sites on FactHound have been researched by our staff.

Here's all you do:

Visit *www.facthound.com*

Type in this code: 9781515746003

 Check out projects, games and lots more at **www.capstonekids.com**

Critical Thinking Using the Common Core

1. Name two parts of the camel's body that help it to live in the desert. Tell how these parts help the camel. (Key Ideas and Details)

2. Read page 18. Why do you think it's important for calves to stand soon after they are born? (Integration of Knowledge and Ideas)

3. Think of another animal that lives in the desert. How is the camel the same or different from that animal? (Craft and Structure)

Index